Collins Primary Science

STORIES

Linda Howe

Resources Needed

Collections To Be Made

Gloves (1)

Sets of big, medium-sized and small objects (5)

Shiny metal objects (2)

General Resources

Art straws (13)

Black paper (8)

Bowls (9)

Card (11,13)

Cardboard boxes (7,13)

Cardboard tubes (11,12,13)

Chalk (4,14)

Clear acetate (11)

Cloth (2)

Construction sets (13)

Cotton wool (1)

Dowel (10)

Dried peas (1)

Feathers (1,7)

Globe (14)

Glue (1,10)

Icing sugar (9)

Iron filings (11)

Knives (9,12)

Leaves (7)

Lentils (1)

Magnets (11)

Mirrors (12)

Newspaper (3)

Paint (12)

Paper (1,2,3,12)

Pastry brush (9)

Pegs (4)

Pencils (1,2,12)

Pipe cleaners (6)

Plasticine (12)

Potting compost (8)

Rice (1)

Scissors (10)

Sewing machine (1)

Shiny paper (12)

Small objects (5,6)

Small pots (8)

Small squares of cloth (1)

Spoons (9)

Straw (7)

Stick (4)

String (4,6)

Wood (3)

Wooden beads (10)

Wrapping paper (5)

Yoghurt pots (10,13)

Other Resources

Apples (3,12)

Biscuits (3,9)

Chocolate (9)

Hot-water bottles (7)

Ping-pong balls (10)

Rice paper (10)

Seeds, packets of different (8)

Slices of bread (8)

Sweets (9)

Contents

	Resources needed	2
1	The Princess and the Pea	4
2	Aladdin	6
3	Sleeping Beauty	8
4	Cinderella	10
5	The Three Bears	12
6	Dick Whittington	14
7	Babes in the Wood	16
8	Jack and the Beanstalk	18
9	Hansel and Gretel	20
10	Alice in Wonderland	22
11	Cinderella again	24
12	Snow White	26
13	Rapunzel	28
14	Stories of the stars	30
	Acknowledgements	32

1 THE PRINCESS AND THE PEA

OBSERVING

Do you know the story of *The Princess and the Pea*? The story tells of a girl who proved that she was a real princess because she could feel a pea through 20 mattresses and 20 quilts.

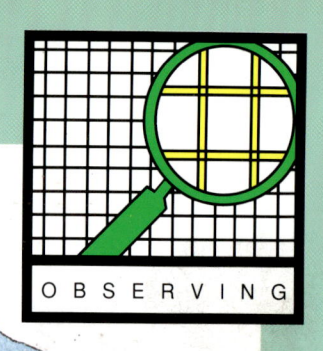

What can you feel through?

YOU NEED

Collection of gloves   Marbles   Rice
Dried peas   Lentils   Cotton wool   Feathers
Small squares of cloth   Glue   Paper   Pencils
Sewing machine if possible

ACTIVITY – A –

Put some things out on the table.
You could try: a marble, a grain of rice, a pea, a feather as well as your own ideas.
Put one square of cloth over each object.
Can you feel the objects through the cloth?
Try putting another square over the top.
Can you still feel the objects?
Continue adding squares of cloth until you no longer feel the objects. Through how many layers of cloth can you feel each one?

RECORDING Show how many layers you could feel the items through.

ACTIVITY – B –

Take two squares of cloth and use them to make a bag. Glue or sew around three sides and then choose something to put inside. It might be: marbles, dried peas, rice, cotton wool or feathers.
Put your objects inside the bag and glue or sew up the fourth side.
Make some more bags in the same way, putting different things inside each.
Feel your bags. What do the objects feel like?
Can a friend guess what is inside by feeling?

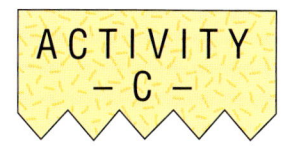

ACTIVITY – C – Write your name on a piece of paper.
Now put a glove or mitten on the hand which you write with and write your name again.
Is it easier or harder to write your name with a glove on?
Try different types of glove. Which is easiest and which is hardest to write with?

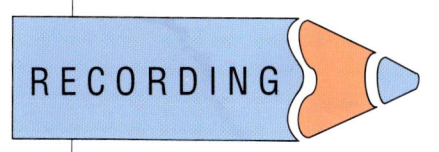

RECORDING Draw a picture of each glove next to your writing.

2 ALADDIN

OBSERVING

In the story of *Aladdin* there is a magic lamp.
When Aladdin rubs the lamp a
genie appears and offers him a wish.
Imagine that you have a magic lamp.
What would your wish be?
Paint a picture of your wish or
act it out with a friend.

What can you find out about shiny things?

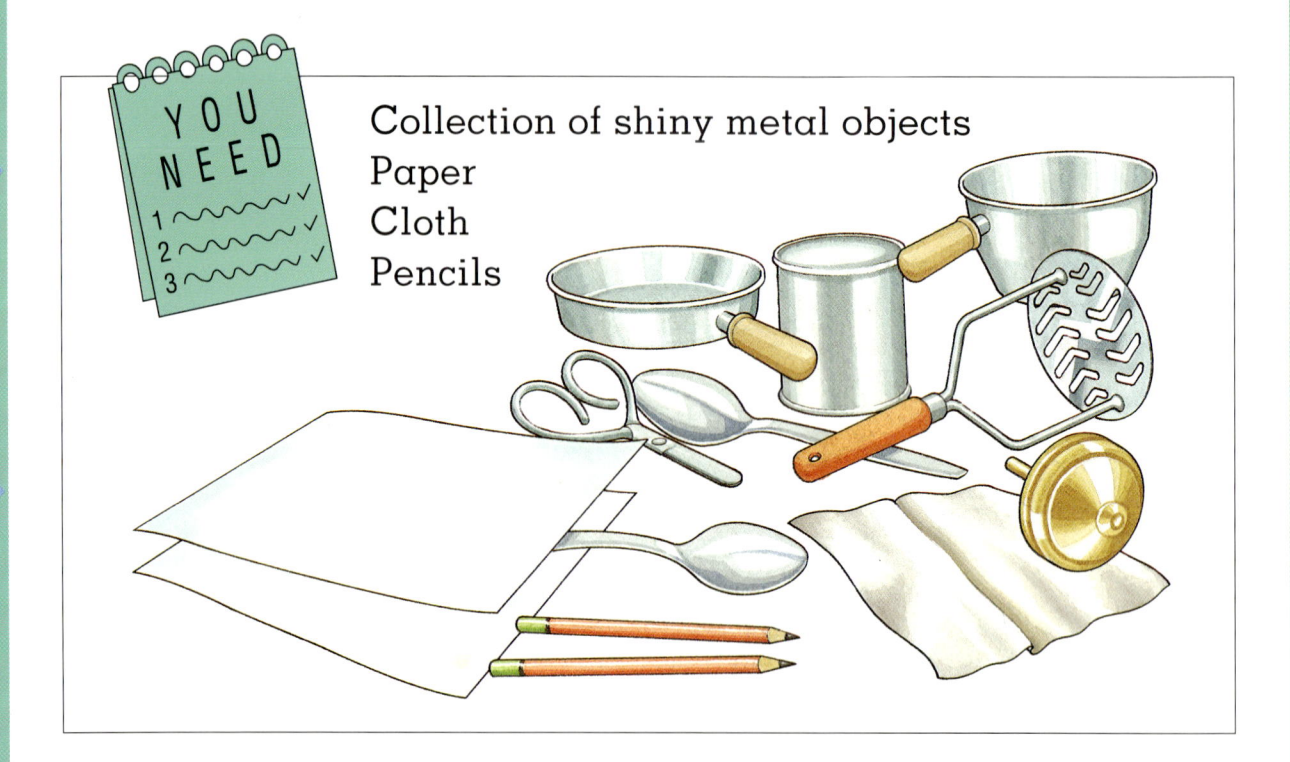

YOU NEED
Collection of shiny metal objects
Paper
Cloth
Pencils

ACTIVITY – A –
Look in the shiny things.
Can you see yourself?
You may need to polish the objects to see yourself clearly.
Do you look the same as you do when you look in a mirror?

How does the object change your reflection?
Try looking in a flat and a curved object.
Try something with holes in.
Which objects make you look different?

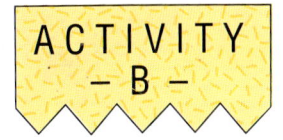

ACTIVITY – B –

Work in two groups.
Everyone should have one of the shiny things, a piece of paper and a pencil.
Look in your shiny thing and draw your reflection as you see it.
Now put all the shiny things in the middle of the table and swap your picture with a picture drawn by someone in the other group.
Everyone should do the same.
Can each group match the drawings they now have to the shiny things on the table?
Which are easiest to match?
Which are most difficult to match?
Can you find any other shiny things to look in?
What can you see your reflection in?

RECORDING

Make a display of shiny things together with your drawings.

3 SLEEPING BEAUTY

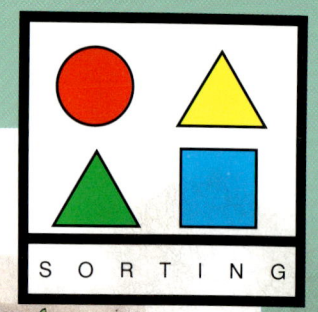

SORTING

Find the story of *Sleeping Beauty* in a book. In the story the princess and everyone else in the castle fall asleep for 100 years. What do you think will have changed when they wake up?

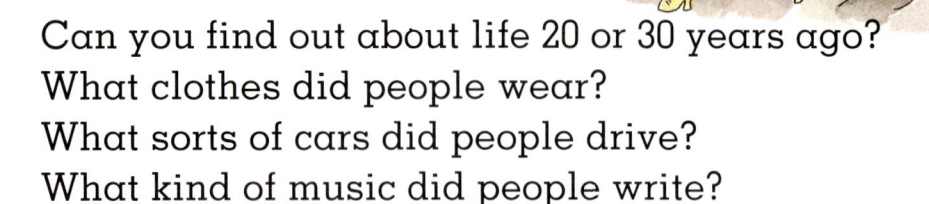

Can you find out about life 20 or 30 years ago?
What clothes did people wear?
What sorts of cars did people drive?
What kind of music did people write?

You might be able to find an old map of the area where your school is.
Look and see if there have been any new houses or roads built since the map was drawn?
When was your school built?
Have any changes been made to the building since then?

How do things change over a week?

YOU NEED

Biscuit
Slice of bread
Apple
Piece of paper
Wood
Newspaper

You must be careful not to touch or taste the food items after you have left them.

ACTIVITY - A -

Put the things you have chosen on a windowsill or a table in the sunlight.
Look at the things and draw them.
You might write some words to help you remember what they are like.

Imagine that you are going to sleep for one week. What do you think the objects will look like when you wake up?
Leave the objects for a week and then look at them.
Have they changed in any way?
You could put your hand in a plastic bag and touch them through the plastic to feel if they are hard or soft.

ACTIVITY - B -

Repeat Activity A but this time put the objects outside and leave them for a week. What might be different about them after the week?
After a week look at the objects.
What has happened to them?

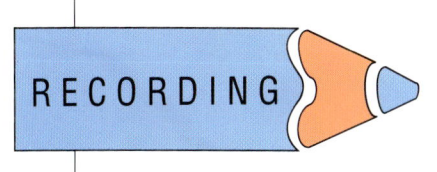

RECORDING

You can draw the objects to show the way they have changed or you could take photographs of them at the beginning and end of the week.

9

4 CINDERELLA

SORTING

In the story of *Cinderella* the fairy godmother tells Cinderella to be home by 12 o'clock. How many different ways of measuring time can you think of?

There are different kinds of clocks:

digital clocks    alarm clocks    grandfather clocks 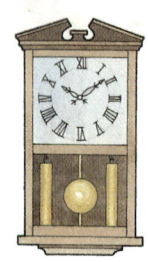   pendulum clocks

Can you think of any others?

Long ago, people used different ways of telling the time. They used:

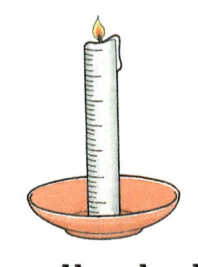

candle clocks 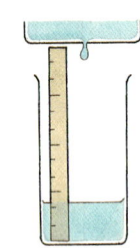   water clocks 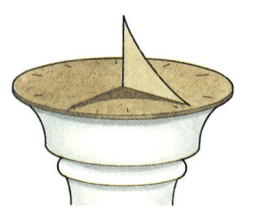   sundials

Can you find out about any other old ways of telling the time?

Can you make a shadow clock?

YOU NEED

Large stick   String   Pegs   Chalk

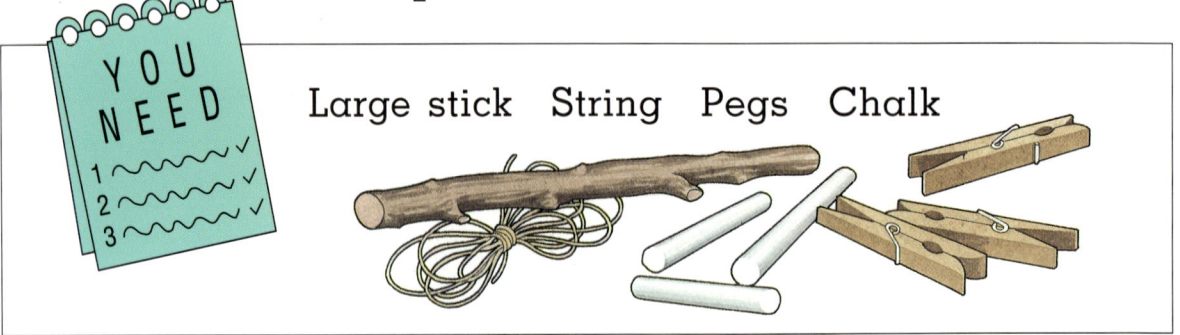

ACTIVITY - A -

Go outside on a sunny morning and look at your shadow. Where do you look to see it? If you turn around does it stay in the same place or does it turn with you?
Is everyone's shadow on the same side?
Look at your shadow at different times of day. What do you notice?

ACTIVITY - B -

Make a shadow clock. Find a space clear of overhanging trees and buildings. Put your stick in the ground or stand it in a bucket of sand on the playground.
Mark where the shadow of the stick is. Mark the shadow every hour.
You can use string and pegs or chalk to mark the shadows.
How many hours can you mark on your shadow clock?
Why is your clock no use at night or on a dull day?
Can you use your clock to tell the time?

RECORDING

Can a friend draw around your shadow at different times of the day? What do you notice about the shadow shapes?

5 THE THREE BEARS

MEASURING

Do you know the story of *The Three Bears*?
There was a great big bear,
a middle-sized bear and a tiny bear.
You could draw or paint a
picture of the three bears,
make some models of
them or use cloth pieces
to make bear shapes.

Can you make collections of different sized things?
Look for big, medium and small:
- bottles
- dolls
- tins
- balls
- books
- toy cars

and your own ideas.

Put your objects in order from big to little.
Can you put all the children in the class into order of size?
Who is the tallest?
Who is the shortest?

Can you sort things for wrapping?

YOU NEED

Sets of three objects (one big, one medium and one small)
Wrapping paper to match the size of the objects
Variety of small objects

ACTIVITY - A -

Work in groups of three. Each group should have three objects; a big one, a medium-sized one and a small one. Each person in the group should have one of the objects.
Put the three sheets of paper in the middle of the group.
Someone should say, "Go" and everyone should start wrapping their objects.
Which group finishes wrapping first?
Do you think that it is best to sort the paper first or for everyone to grab a piece?
Change objects with another group and try again.
Are you quicker this time?

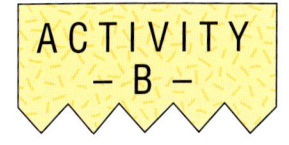

ACTIVITY - B -

Smooth out the pieces of wrapping paper.
How many small things will the smallest piece wrap?
Can you estimate how many things the other two pieces will wrap?
Try the medium piece and then the small piece. How close were your estimations?

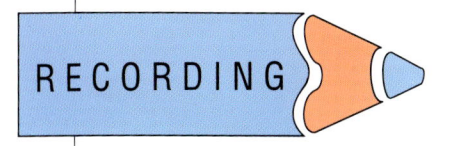

RECORDING

Show your estimations and results on a chart.

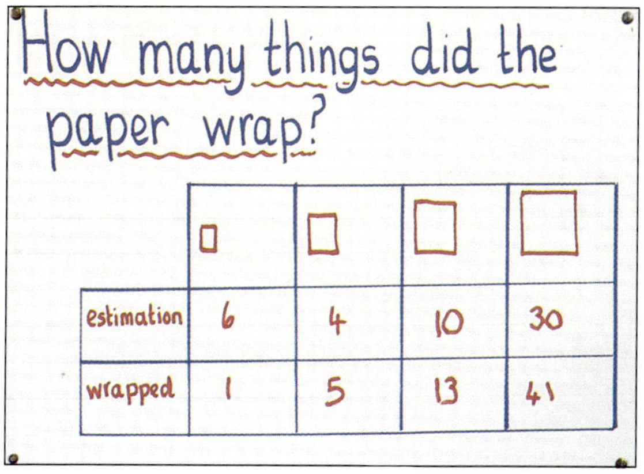

How many things did the paper wrap?

	□	□	□	□
estimation	6	4	10	30
wrapped	1	5	13	41

6 DICK WHITTINGTON

Find the story of *Dick Whittington* to read. When Dick goes to London he wraps all his things in a bundle and ties it to a stick to carry.

If you were going on a long walk how would you carry your things? Would you put them in:

- a suitcase?
- a bag or basket?
- a box?

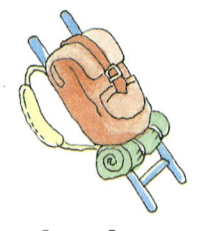

- a back pack?
- a cart?
- a wheelbarrow?

Think of some other ways to carry things.

How many things can you wrap in a bundle?

YOU NEED

Different size pieces of cloth and different kinds of cloth cut to the same size
String   Large pipe cleaners   Small objects

ACTIVITY -A-

Choose three different size pieces of cloth. Take the smallest and estimate how many things you can wrap in it.
See how many objects you can wrap and still be able to tie up the bundle with string or a pipe cleaner.
Now try the other two pieces.
For each one estimate and then try.
Do you get better at estimating?

ACTIVITY -B-

Choose three different kinds of cloth. The pieces must be the same size. Take one piece and estimate how many things it will wrap and then try to see if you were right.

Do you think that the other two pieces will wrap the same number of things? Try and see if they do.

Can you think of any reasons why they might not wrap the same number of things?

RECORDING

Show your results on a chart.

7 BABES IN THE WOOD

FAIR TESTING

The story of *Babes in the Wood* tells us about two children who have to keep themselves warm in a wood.

They might use: leaves, twigs, feathers or dry grass to help them keep warm?.
Can you think of anything else they might find?

How do you keep warm at night?
Do you wear pyjamas, a nightshirt or a nightdress?
Do you have a heater in your bedroom?
Do you use blankets, a quilt or a duvet?
What else do you have on your bed?

If you were going to spend a night camping what would you use to keep warm?

Birds try to make their nests using things that will help keep their chicks warm.

Can you make a warm nest?

YOU NEED

Hot-water bottle for each group
Straw   Leaves   Feathers   Sheep's wool   Twigs
Large cardboard box for each group

16

ACTIVITY

Work with a group of friends. Try to make a nest to keep your hot-water bottle warm. You can make your nest in a cardboard box.

Before you start to make your nest talk about:
- what you will use
- how you will make your nest
- which people in the group will do the different jobs

Now make your nest using some of the materials you have collected.

When all the groups' nests are ready put a warm hot-water bottle in each. How long will you leave them for? You might try half an hour or an hour.

After that time feel the bottles.

Are they all still warm?

Are some still warm?

Are they all cold?

You can check the temperature by feeling or you may be able to use a thermometer.

Which do you think is the best nest?

RECORDING

Write down what you used to make your nest and how good you think it was.

JACK AND THE BEANSTALK

FAIR TESTING

In the story of *Jack and the Beanstalk* Jack's mother throws some beans into the garden. They are magic beans and an enormous beanstalk grows up in the night.

Imagine that you wake up one morning and see an enormous beanstalk growing outside your window. It is so tall that you cannot see the top of it. You start to climb up the beanstalk. It is a hard climb but after a while you reach the top and find yourself in the land of dinosaurs.

Can you find some books to help you find out the names of some dinosaurs, their size and what they ate? You could choose one dinosaur and find out as much as you can about it. What has changed since the time of dinosaurs?
What would happen if you took a dinosaur home with you?

Can you find out about any other animals or creatures that have died out?

Do all seeds like the same growing conditions?

YOU NEED

Packet of seeds of different varieties
Small pots
Potting compost
Black paper
Labels

ACTIVITY -A-

Can you test to find out where seeds grow best?
Plant your seeds in small pots and put some of each type in a different place.
You could try putting them in the dark, near a heater and in a refrigerator as well as trying your own ideas.
Which seeds appear first?
Which grow slowly?
Which don't grow?

RECORDING

Write down the best conditions for each kind of seed.

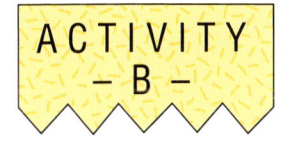

ACTIVITY -B-

Do beans need light and water to grow?
Plant some beans in pots.
Water some of the pots but leave one or two dry.
Cover some with black paper.
Make a small hole in the paper covering of one or two.
Which beans grow best?

RECORDING

Make labels to say how the beans were treated and if they grew or not.

9 HANSEL AND GRETEL

Do you know the story of *Hansel and Gretel*? In the story a witch lives in a gingerbread house. If you were going to make a house using things that you can eat what would you use?

Draw or paint a picture of your house. What will you use for:

- the roof?
- the chimney pot?
- the walls?
- the windows?
- the doors?

What will you use to hold your house together? You could try icing, butter, chocolate, tomato ketchup or your own ideas.

Can you make an edible house?

YOU NEED

Icing sugar   Rice paper   Sweets   Biscuits
Pastry brush   Chocolate   Spoons   Bowls   Knives

ACTIVITY - A -

Can you make a house picture that you can eat? Mix some icing sugar with a little water for your glue.
Take a piece of rice paper and some sweets. Can you use the sweets to make a house picture? Plan your picture first and when you are ready use the pastry brush to glue your sweets to the rice paper.
Let your picture dry and then you can eat it.

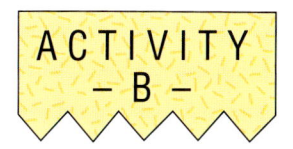

ACTIVITY - B -

Can you find out what joins biscuits together best? Take four biscuits.
Use the icing sugar glue to stick two of the biscuits together.
Melt the chocolate and use this to stick two more biscuits together.
Let them dry and then see which you think are stuck together the best. You can eat the biscuits.

RECORDING

Photographs form the best record of this activity.

10 ALICE IN WONDERLAND

In the story of *Alice in Wonderland* Alice finds that when she drinks from a bottle she gets smaller and smaller but when she eats a cake she gets taller.

What do you think it would be like if you were smaller or taller? Make a list of things that you can see now and then a list of things that you would see if you were much taller.

Lie on the floor and look up. What would things look like if you were much smaller?
You could draw or paint a picture of what things look like from the floor.
Do things look very tall?
Do you see the underside or the top of them?

Think of a small animal. It could be:
- a mouse
- a worm
- an ant
- a spider

What do you think it can see?

Can you make a figure to grow taller and smaller?

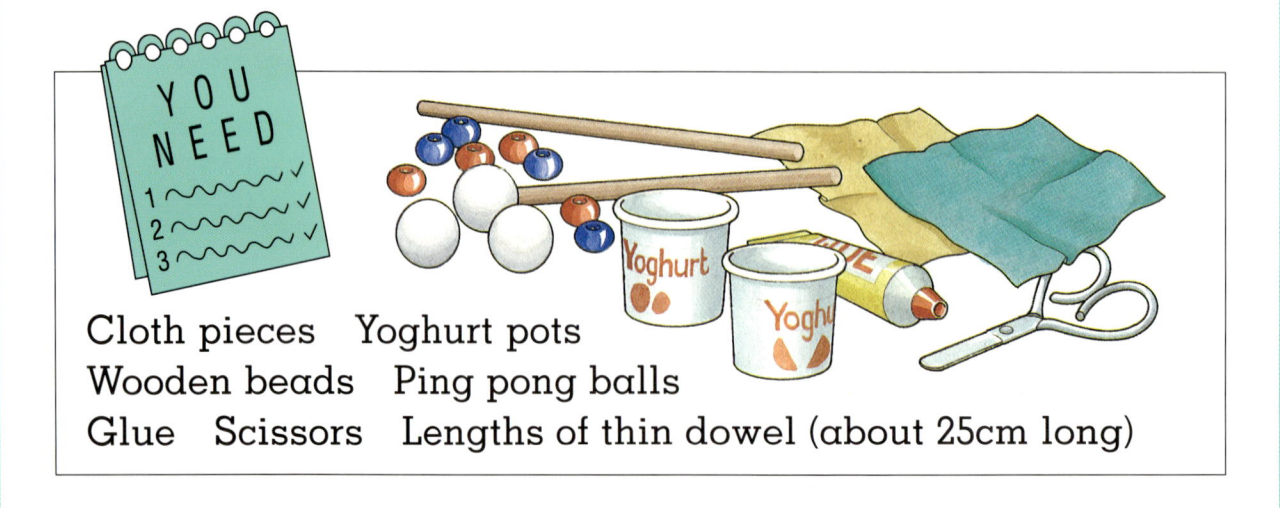

YOU NEED

Cloth pieces   Yoghurt pots
Wooden beads   Ping pong balls
Glue   Scissors   Lengths of thin dowel (about 25cm long)

ACTIVITY

Ask an adult to help you make a hole in the bottom of your yoghurt pot. It must be big enough to let the dowel go through and for it to move easily.
Stick the ball or bead on one end of the dowel.
Cut a large circle of cloth (about 30cm diameter) and make a hole in the centre of the cloth.
Put the dowel through and stick the cloth under the ball.
Push the yoghurt pot onto the dowel and stick the edges of the cloth to the top of the pot.
When you move the dowel up and down the bead should also move up and down.
Decorate your figure. You could draw or paint eyes, a nose and mouth, add wool hair as well as your own ideas.

RECORDING Either display the finished figures or photographs of them.

11 CINDERELLA AGAIN

In the story of *Cinderella* the fairy godmother helps to change Cinderella's old clothes into a ballgown. Can you remember some other things that she changes?

Fold a piece of paper in half. On one side draw Cinderella in an old dress and on the other side draw her in a ballgown. How many differences are there between the two pictures? What is the same in both pictures?

Draw some more changing pictures. You could draw:
- a house in summer and winter
- you at school and at home
- a daytime and a night-time picture
- a calm day and a windy day
- a happy person and a sad person

as well as your own ideas.

For each pair of pictures find how many differences there are. Change with a friend and find the differences in their pictures.

Can you make a changing face?

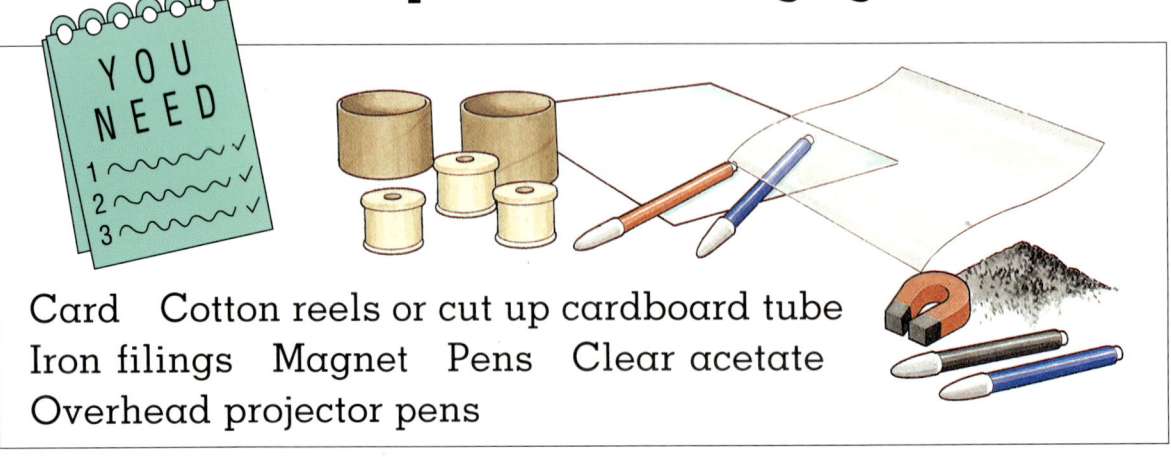

YOU NEED

Card   Cotton reels or cut up cardboard tube
Iron filings   Magnet   Pens   Clear acetate
Overhead projector pens

ACTIVITY - A -

Draw a face on a piece of card but do not give it any hair. Put the piece of card on top of four cotton reels or sections of cardboard tube. Sprinkle iron filings onto the face. Can you use the magnet underneath the card to make different "hair styles" with the iron filings? Do not let the magnet touch the iron filings.
Can you make any other pictures in the same way? You could try a hedgehog with moving spikes or a bird with moving feathers.

ACTIVITY - B -

Can you make an identikit picture?
Draw the outline of a face on one sheet of acetate. Draw some eyes on another, a nose on the next sheet and mouth on the next. What does your face look like? Work with a friend and see how many different faces you can make between you.

RECORDING Make two drawings to show how the same shape of face can have different features.

12 SNOW WHITE

DESIGNING

In the story of *Snow White* the Queen has a magic mirror which tells her who is the most beautiful lady in the land. She is vain and hopes that the mirror will tell her that she is the most beautiful lady. Read the story to find out what happens.

What can you find out about mirrors?

YOU NEED

Apples   Mirrors
Shiny gold/silver paper
Card cylinders
Plasticine   Pencils
Paint   Felt pens
Paper   Knife

ACTIVITY – A –

Work with a group of friends.
Take a mirror and cut an apple in half.
Can you use the mirror to make the apple whole again?
Now cut one half of the the apple in half again.
Can you use mirrors to make this quarter apple whole again?
Can you use the Plasticine to design your own shapes to cut up and use a mirror to make them whole again?
Does it make any difference where you cut your shapes?

ACTIVITY - B -

Can you make these half-pictures whole using a mirror?

fish

person

butterfly

snake

flower

Do you have to be careful where you put the mirror?
What happens with these pictures?
Why do you get unusual shapes?
Now draw some of your own pictures.

ACTIVITY - C -

Make some mirror patterns.
Paint a multi-coloured "blob" on a piece of paper. When it is dry put a mirror on it and turn the mirror round. What do you see?
Try some other patterns.
You could try making a thick, wavy line and putting a mirror on it.
Slide the mirror backwards and forwards. What do you notice?
Wrap some shiny paper around a card tube.
Turn this on your patterns. What do you see now?

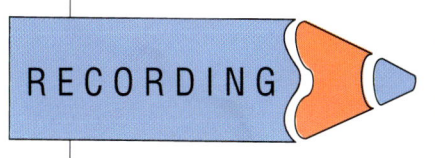

RECORDING

Tell someone else what you have found out.

13 RAPUNZEL

In the story of *Rapunzel* the witch imprisons Rapunzel in a very tall tower. A prince visits her by climbing up her long hair.

INVESTIGATING

Who can build the tallest tower?

YOU NEED

Different construction sets
Art straws   Card   Boxes
Cylindrical containers   Yoghurt pots

ACTIVITY

Work in groups to find out how many different ways you can build a tall tower.
Which group can find the most ways to build the tallest tower?
Which tower stands the straightest?

RECORDING

Measure each tower with a piece of string and make a chart to show how tall they are.

How strong is hair?

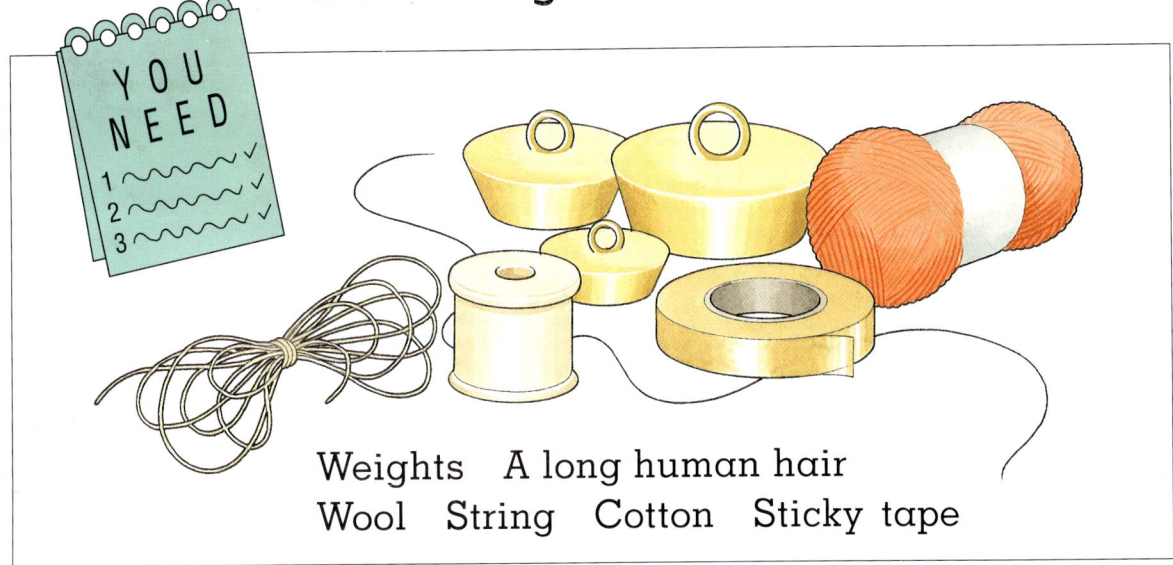

YOU NEED

Weights   A long human hair
Wool   String   Cotton   Sticky tape

ACTIVITY

Can you find out how strong a hair is?
Put the weights in order from the heaviest to the lightest.
Take the lightest weight and use sticky tape to join it to one end of the hair.
Pick up the other end of the hair. Is it strong enough to lift the weight?
Keep trying bigger weights until the hair breaks.
What will it lift?
Now try some of the other things. What will they lift?
Will they lift more or less than the hair?
Do you think that they are stronger or not as strong as the hair?

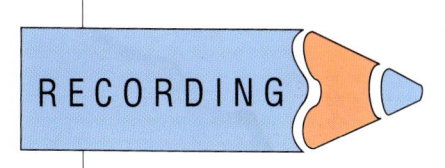

RECORDING

Stick a piece of everything you used on a chart showing the weight that each picked up.

STORIES OF THE STARS

INVESTIGATING

Long ago people made up stories about the sun, the moon and the stars in the sky.

Native Americans told stories about a family. The sun was the father and moon was the mother. The stars were children who were frightened of the father so they ran away when he came out.
Every month the sun catches some of the stars. This makes the moon sad so she covers her face. The moon slowly uncovers her face so that by the end of the month you can see all of it again.

What can you find out about the earth, sun, moon and stars?

YOU NEED

Ball or globe
Lamp without a shade
Chalk

Remember that it is not safe to look at the sun.

ACTIVITY - A -

The earth is like a giant ball. You might be able to look at a globe and find where you live on it.

The earth turns slowly round.
Put your finger on a ball or a globe.
Turn the ball or globe until your finger is back where it started from.
The earth turns round like this once every day.
How many times does it turn in a week?

ACTIVITY - B -

Put the lamp on and hold the ball or globe next to it.
Does it shine on all of the ball or only on part of it?
Make a chalk cross on the ball or globe.
Hold the globe next to the bulb and turn it round slowly once.
When is the cross in the light and when is it in the dark?
If the ball or globe was the earth and the lamp was the sun when do you think it would be night?

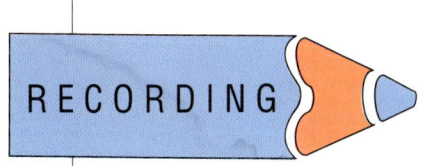

RECORDING

You might be able to look at the night sky and draw some of the star patterns you see.

Acknowledgements

Copyright © 1990 Linda Howe
ISBN 0 00 317564 2

Published by Collins Educational
77–85 Fulham Palace Road
Hammersmith London W6 8JB
This edition 1992
Designed by Shireen Nathoo
Illustrations by Sally Neave and Jo Wright (The Gallery)
Covers by Liz Daniel
Commissioned Photography by Oliver Hatch
Picture Research by Gwenan Morgan

Typeset by Kalligraphic Design Ltd., Horley, Surrey
Printed and bound in Hong Kong

All rights reserved. No part of this book may be
reproduced or transmitted in any form or by any
means, without the prior permission of the publisher.

The publishers thank Woodlands Park Junior School,
London and Woolpit County Primary School,
Suffolk for their kind co-operation in the production of
Collins Primary Science Key Stage 1, Set Two.